CW01431994

SMART BUDGETING FOR SINGLE PARENTS

SMART BUDGETING FOR SINGLE PARENTS

Making Every Penny Count

AVERY NIGHTINGALE

Creative Quill Press

CONTENTS

CHAPTER 1

Introduction

Time and love are immeasurable; no method of budgeting would work for them. But because we are discussing what the smart single parent can do, I will stress the importance of making the most of all the precious moments you have with your family. Notice that although living expenses are necessary, I listed them as the least important of the described essentials. This is because all of it is just stuff. Never substitute it for quality time with your child. Don't worry, I will show you how to manage all the other listed essentials so that together you and yours can share the best of every day in a healthy, safe environment in uncharted lands. Become an explorer of life and a teacher of many things!

This Book is intended to help you examine your personal situation and provide you with a budget plan that will enable you to have a better life as a single parent. It is based on personal past and current experiences and may not entirely apply to every parent, but it is meant to serve as a guideline. So let's begin with the basics. Time, love, care, and support are the elements that outweigh all others when it comes to parenting. Great, you have that (I'm sure), but life also comes with its other essentials: bills. For our purposes, they can be classified as bills, loans, and living expenses, with a further breakdown into other categories. We will discuss each of these elements and why attention is necessary for each of them.

CHAPTER 2

Understanding the Importance of Budgeting

If you use the information in your budget to save yourself from making a single purchase you would later regret – you're truly using a budget to gain control of your spending habits. Anyone can just create a budget – but it's another thing to examine yourself, learn from yourself, and change yourself. I don't think anyone can really escape not creating a budget – at some point, we all need a clearer understanding of income and spending habits. It's one thing to budget when you have a single income and are making an honest attempt to get control of a bad situation. Things are entirely different when you're trying to tell yourself that everything is under control while hiding a mess of unwise spending choices and financial irresponsibility; that's not budgeting – that would be called denial.

1. Making a budget 2) Using the budget to truly understand your spending habits 3) Using the understanding you gain about your spending habits in making your next budget 4) Actually living on a budget

Learning to budget correctly is perhaps the best thing you can do to understand your finances and control your spending. Budgeting used to mean "making a budget," which probably sounds like a punishment of some sort. But in fact, making the budget is just the very first step. The progression of learning to budget goes like this:

Assessing Your Financial Situation
Smart strategy: Budget for income and expenses on a monthly basis, because that's how most people pay for goods and services. Some expenses, especially bills, are monthly, but others are paid annually (like insurance) or weekly (like outreach activities), so you may need to prorate these costs in your monthly budget. It can help to create a separate monthly budget for each category of regular expenses. This can be a smart tool to help you manage tight finances, to spot high costs that might be reduced, and to help plan for the future. You can adjust your budget as you become more skilled and confident. Over time, experience will help you see how to deal with the irregular expenses and cash flow in your family's budget. Soon you may need only one budget for all household expenses, updated each month, although the individual monthly budgets may still help you make regular family decisions.
Look at income versus expenses. A budget is a plan that helps you manage the money you have coming in against the things you need to spend it on. Start with the regular income and regular monthly expenses of your household and assign every dollar to a particular category. Some people still use the "envelope" budget: literally putting cash into various envelopes marked for each budget area, a visible reminder of your financial "floor". Others use a notepad, computer program, or spreadsheet to organize the amounts. The computer or other

living expenses need to be spent from those envelopes. Record and track all your spending, and when the cash is gone, stop spending!

Setting Financial Goals

The first step to setting financial goals is getting more specific than just saying that you want better finances. What does better finances really mean? What does that look like to you? For example, a traveling goal might be, "I want to be able to plan several special vacations for my family in the next three years." Build your goals and objectives around SMART goals, which are specific, measurable, attainable, relevant, and time-bound. Setting SMART goals involves fully understanding the goal (Specific), having a method to measure progress toward the goal (Measurable), ensuring that the goal is important to you to help keep you on track (Attainable), considering focus and other goals that are important to you (Relevant), and having deadlines for when you want to achieve the goal (Time-bound). When you apply these principles as you set your goals, you will have an easy time accomplishing them with few setbacks or financial troubles while maintaining smart budgeting practices because the two tend to work together.

Having an understanding of your financial situation helps you to know where you are in terms of your financial position, and from there, you can establish your financial objectives or goals for the future. Goals are useful in helping you to manage your personal finances, and one area is physical planning and budgeting. Setting financial goals is a key part of personal finance planning and personal financial success. Personal finance software helps you to look at your financial goals and plan right. In this article, you'll learn how to set financial goals and use personal finance tools to improve and manage your personal finance.

Creating a Realistic Budget

The budget should balance income with expenses, interest, principal payments, taxes, and capital investments. It should account for inflation and taxation. It should be responsive to new changes in family size, number and cost of children, number of working parents and caregivers, health insurance, education needs and expenses, holidays, home repairs and maintenance, as well as emergency and development needs.

It should include the regular, mandatory, and voluntary payments, the maintenance, saving and investment, servicing, emergency, insurance, entertainment, and giving amount as well. It should also account for legal judgments, wage reduction, and layoff, loan defaults, government entitlement, overtime adjustments, investments, as well as small business capital. What it should not account for is market changes, government inflation or war, sustainable unemployment, large investments in market speculation, constant increases in grocery, utility, and gasoline prices, build out of trust funds, friends and family savings, severance or paycheck windfalls, stock dividends, gifts payouts, Ponzi scheme, or business run out of a manila envelope.

Creating a budget engenders personal discipline and responsibility to understanding your spending, knowing the amount the children have available for them to enjoy as a family, and also to set priorities and make adjustments as much as necessary. The most important thing is to start the process right away. No matter what the surprise or what the income-producing activity, living on your budget should be your first priority. That is right, you should try and live on your budget while you are setting up your budget guideline.

Creating a realistic budget is the most important step in developing the financial strategy that will guarantee peace of mind for you and your children. The budget is a fundamental family financial plan because it helps you measure where you are in relation to your goals, set targets, and monitor your success. It is the accountability tool for intelligent money management. It is also the best way to plan your spending amounts without borrowing, start saving, invest with no risk, and live within your means.

Tracking Your Expenses

Where you can, substitute eating out with home-cooked meals: a $10 lunch becomes $2.50 easily (my girls really love Chinese lo mein, I make them for $0.50 a serving—basically a plate). Outdoor movie with snacks and popcorn: we rent a DVD and make our own popcorn. An extracurricular swimming event is a once-in-a-month outing, at the same time I get to swim with them. We started our own odd system of reward. Once in two to three months, if our savings budget meets our expectation, we treat ourselves to dinner at a simple and inexpensive buffet restaurant. If any of the kids need to see a movie, we wait for the DVD release and rent one, with some junk food of course. And typically we meet our quarterly reward; my kids are happy.

One way to keep these costs low is to avoid the temptations associated with a consumer lifestyle. Peer pressure is strong, and you want to fit in. Now your focus should be surviving and managing your special financial responsibility. One way to keep costs at a minimum is to become minimalist, that is, avoid collecting material possessions.

Understandably, budgeting and tracking will not uncover fees and expenses that are difficult to count, e.g., evening out with coworkers after work, impromptu lunchtime delivery from your favorite restaurant, or a pop-up sale on your way home. These impromptu expenses are variable, fluctuating, and could pose a massive challenge to your budgeting and financial tracking. These are pitfalls in your budgeting effort; ignore them and a beyond meager discretionary income becomes an unattainable reality.

Saving Strategies

Every little bit of cash I find, I put into the bank, normally for family outings and activities. Grocery shopping also helps. Rewards, free money...whatever you want to call it, I take it. For shopping trips, I help the kids deposit their coins into our free coin-counting machine at the bank about twice a year, and then we take it out of the children's carnival prize pond or use it for a movie or dinner. Then, of course, there is the two-week rule: If I don't want or need something bad enough to buy it right then or don't really need to purchase it in urgency, I make myself wait to see if I still want it in two weeks. Usually, I don't. This rule has saved me countless dollars.

At the store: Did I mention thrift stores? I'll say it again: They aren't all filled with broken yard-sale cast-offs. I've found them to be a goldmine of like-new clothes for the kids and me at a fraction of new retail costs. I bought a beautiful, rainbow-striped prom dress for my daughter that looked as if it had come from Nordstrom for $10. At a local store not too long ago, I found a BCBG Max Azria jeans outfit that looked like it had been on the rack for a year or two (it's silver and orange), still with the original tags for under $20. Crazy! When new things go on clearance, I check online to see if I can find discount codes and free shipping codes to make it an even better deal. I find a lot of deals at Overstock. If you join their club, you pay an annual fee and your shipping is always just $2.95. No kidding.

Maximizing Income Opportunities

Paying for work with children: Nobody will be more interested in how a new contract or hiring decision will impact children and cash benefits in the short term than a single father or mother. Working mothers plainly say that if they have any money left once they have paid for child care, there is more incentive for them to work. The most suitable situation for children is when family effectiveness is improved by working caregivers. Usually, those caregivers are the children's parents. Unfortunately, for a generation already, there will be intergenerational damage resulting from our collapse of engagement in the work that helps children.

Maximizing income: Along with controlling costs, single parents can significantly expand their net budgets through earning increases. Usually, parents create their main earning source through their work (and possibly through government aid). They should be devoted to improving their earning abilities. There are multiple possibilities for this, such as improving research and job-seeking abilities, obtaining in-demand market skills. Research has shown that for both female-headed and male-headed families, improving the mother's earnings is important, providing the greatest economic advantages. Working overtime or finding a better job can also be an important source of income.

Managing Debt

In my previous book, we deliberated about budgeting, and trying to be good at it. We also touched upon understanding economic predators. It takes skill, knowledge, diligence, caution, patience, and persistence to get it right. It is thrilling to write about the power of budgeting. A great wealth of readily available information is devoted to stretching every single dollar until it is about to burst. Topics usually include "the 10 best ways to save money", "the five best never before published budgeting tips", "what mustn't you forget if you earn less than...10000". Such themes provide almost an instant savings boost, incentive, praise, and assurance that at least something useful is being done. What can be a sweeter incentive to go on than reading some "quick savings fixes"? Unfortunately, articles of that kind may lead to savings burnout, not because of the tips - some of them are really good, but because of a radical approach to savings in which "some smart saving tactics are fine but lots are much better".

Have you ever wondered what kind of attitude most single parents have towards budgeting, savings, and debt? Even though it may be difficult to imagine an exact ratio of people in distinct categories, such an inquiry on my website has shown that single parents are overwhelming in the following categories: (1) do not ever budget, and if they ever attempt at doing that, such attempts eventually lead to failure, (2) consume more than they should, (3) have difficulty in saving, and (4) carry a lot of debt - excluding the education mortgage or loan. As much as 85.71% of single parents do not budget; 76.19% overspend; 71.43% do not save; and a whopping 90.48% possess a lot of debt.

Prioritizing Essential Expenses

Once you've gathered the numbers, you need to make sure you are prioritizing the necessary expenses. This crucial step involves revisiting the budget, using the numbers as a guideline and your reality as the lens through which you leave, weigh, and layer critical expenses, such as housing, food, and clothing. Arrange your revised budget to consider any child support or alimony payments as necessary tools to keep your family on track. Limit the possibility of miscommunications and misinterpretations about who will pay what bills by specifying and documenting these payments. Make sure to declare that such payments are tax-deductible and are not themselves taxable, schedule and pay on time, and then store the physical receipts in a safe, easily accessible place. You may also want to consider getting some on-the-job training in maintaining a habit of financial accountability through family budgeting or bookkeeping, especially if you will be transitioning back into the workforce. After having cared for home and family for years, adapting to the working world's sometimes unfamiliar pace can be challenging enough, but to do so on the heels of a difficult divorce makes the change particularly acute.

Acknowledging your financial reality can help you establish and maintain your perspective as you move through the next focused steps. Such honesty may also be necessary to ensure that any financial support you were awarded in the divorce settlement is maximized and then utilized in the ways that you've suggested that it be used. Defer to the court documents or agreements for specifics, and also remember to document how you utilized this money. Without this document, there's nothing to stop your former partner from suggesting that you misused the money. Qualifying everything with "mom said" is one of the most pointless exercises in parenting, but in this one instance, you should drive yourself nuts repeating who said what why.

Cutting Back on Non-Essential Expenses

To save money on items that we want to spend less on, my number one tip is to shop only at discount retailers. I've mentioned buying used items before, and using this strategy allowed me to buy only the things I could afford to purchase used, resulting in many trips to thrift stores and garage sales. I also bought plenty of things at discount retailers, and of course bargain shopped. Here is a list of places I shopped at regularly: Discount store (I shopped here most often), big-box store where you can make your clothing shop pull double duty by getting food there, food stores with in-store clothing sections, discount, big-box, or overstock store for clothing, credit card programs that took cash spending and translated it into points or money back to accumulate over the year. When I shopped at regular price stores, I always made sure to bargain shop, never pay full price, and every item I purchased had to be something I absolutely loved.

Don't be afraid to get rid of the "extras." People spend a lot on things they don't really need. Examples of non-essential expenses include expensive cable TV packages, gym memberships (there are free workouts available on YouTube), eating out, and so on. I'm not suggesting that you eliminate every little treat. You're allowed "extras" sometimes. But by cutting back on the things you don't really need to spend money on, you will have more to spend on the things you do. Everybody has different priorities, and what is an extra for you might be a necessity for another. It's okay to enjoy a latte, for instance, because it's a matter of personal priorities. I introduce the concept of priority-based budgeting, which means we go beyond tracking what we spent and categorizing it according to typical budget categories. You can break your budget categories down further so you can see exactly how much you spend per week (or per month) on things that are only important to you.

Meal Planning on a Budget

Planned, guided, and strong financial management can prevent defaults in the fulfillment of regular, recurring mandates in everyday life and ensure a controlled and desired higher lifestyle investment during Nutrition Week. Parents experience consistent failures and discouragement in maintaining a balanced diet plan due to unforeseen costs incurred in the process of strengthening of goals and means. The purpose of the mission gets lost and it looks like the sole responsibility is entirely to blame. Hitherto, economic planning and frugal options become the right approach to create a harmonious balance between short-term parameters and long-term projects. Mid- to prosperous families can afford to stick to the concept of steady progress. Quoting quotes from local market managers, fruit managers, and the sound way presented grants, Picture of Health Vacation Plan: A professional typically requiring a monthly investment of Rs 1500-3000. That extra rupees 200-10,000 will hamper the implementation of a well-planned and justified nutrition schedule without adequate monthly stable resources for training and meal planning.

The complexities of single parenting do not end at the end of the day. When we add the task of meal planning and everyday feeding for a family, stress doubles. Nevertheless, the required level of personal finance and frugal strategy increases significantly. When the concept of single parents juggling and caring for a multigenerational family came up during the city mundan travels or the dreams of a multi-faceted dream house, detailed meal planning on tight budgets was painful and exclusive became. In reality, imported fruits and fresh vegetables have always been secured, but nutritious food has not. Nutrition Week is ongoing and its timing is well planned.

Smart Shopping Tips

Of course, when you have the rare, TWO HOUR time slot known as "grandma's watching him/her," and they're asleep simultaneously, you sprint through the aisles like your feet are on fire. If I suddenly have two hours of freedom, it's a result of missing them while my son was in Sunday School at 9:00 am, and having two hours to work before choir practice. In which case, the budgeting must get done and deposit in the bank before 9:00, and I don't even notice the wait, because I enjoy prioritizing to make the best use of my time. So, if I say you won't use coupons because you don't have two hours once a week, I'm not trying to be funny. I'm being very real on how we work. I will grab a Sunday newspaper, clip a few (1-2) diaper coupons, maybe a yogurt coupon and that's it. Then, I'll grab a Diet Dr. Pepper because it makes me happy, and I need that as much as possible. Then sprint off again. Hire someone to clean for you once a month. Offer to trade a mom of two for cleaning and babysitting services. You deserve it, and the alone time is invaluable. This offers a win/win for both.

Put the coupons down, single parents. It's not that you don't deserve the fifty cents off. You just don't have the time.

Instead, budget shop. My number one grocery shopping rule is against buying toiletries at grocery stores. I compare prices between the grocery store, Big Lots and Walmart, as well as the family-owned cash and carries, and the specialty stores nearby, but now less frequently. At my Big Lots, a four-pack of Noxzema razors is only $2.50, compared to the same for $5 at the Walmart right down the street. Giant rolls of Darwin toilet paper are only $4.50 and their Value-Pack wet wipes are half the cost at $2.75 per pack. I'll buy a small bottle of cheap, $2 V05 conditioner for my daughter's tangly curls, instead of the $3 Pantene conditioner that gets used up twice as fast.

Saving on Utilities

2. Only fill the coffeepot halfway with water if that's all the coffee you want to make. You'll use less electricity running it.

CHAPTER 3

1. Take showers instead of baths. A long shower takes less water than you'd use filling your bathtub.

Older electrical systems allow electricity to escape from open electrical sockets, but you can seal your electrical plugs with simple-to-do "Safe Plug" outlet plugs. Draw the drapes at night too, to keep the warmth in your room. And those plastic strips and plastic plugs for electrical sockets are other items that your hardware department salesman might never have mentioned to you at all. Here are a few other energy-saving tips to give your utility bills a bit of immediate downsizing:

Tremper says shoppers who spend less than $100 in a second-hand store are most satisfied with their purchases.

Families that are "just getting by" may find it difficult to save money in an emergency fund, much less save for retirement or college. After all, if your budget is stretched to its breaking point, there's little room for additional savings. What's a single parent to do? The good news is that kids - especially little kids - don't cost that much as long as you have time to spend. Consider clothing and footwear, for example: They wear their kids just like we do, but kids keep growing night and day and right before our very eyes! Shopping at second-hand stores for children's items makes great sense. Everything looks practically brand new. And, while you probably won't find these at a second-hand store, or make them yourself, consider purchasing a few for yourself as well:

CHAPTER 4

Affordable Housing Options

If you are a working single mother, you may not think Section 8 will benefit your family. However, in many states, income-restricted, affordable housing is available to employed families. Start your search at and contact your state's department of housing or community development for additional information about Section 8 housing in your community. Save money by taking in a roommate. Adding a tenant to your household could put more money in your pocket and provide companionship for both you and your child. Before you put out an ad, discuss the arrangement with a trusted friend and your child in order to avoid problems. If friends or family members who are struggling to make ends meet are not ready to make a commitment, search for a tenant on websites such as Craigslist or MyNewPlace.com. Be sure to check references and conduct a background check on tenants.

One of a single parent's biggest expenses is rent or a mortgage. Even if you rented your first apartment as a single person and thought you were living frugally, the cost of rent can easily double when you add a child. If moving back in with your parents or in-laws is not an option, and you do not want to move to a cheaper neighborhood because you do not want to uproot your child, start looking for the following affordable housing options. Look for sub-sidized housing programs for low-income families. Visit the United States Department of Housing and Urban Development's (HUD) website and check your own state's website for information on federal and state programs. A little research and a lot of paperwork could cut your costs by hundreds of dollars a month. For additional information about housing benefits, contact a local public housing agency.

CHAPTER 5

Childcare Cost Reduction

If you can't find somebody willing to swap childcare, you might be able to save money by hiring a private caregiver, rather than sending your child to a facility-based daycare. To save even more on childcare, I've proposed the plan mentioned earlier, which is of such ingeniously manipulating numbers that it could result in overall savings each time you crunch those figures. These potential savings (hence, equally awesome hack) are due to the fact that private caregivers who work in your home or theirs, still, often charge less than most child care facilities. Some private caregivers refuse to claim income or report it to the IRS. Why is this relevant to YOU? Their lower overhead usually translates into lower costs than what many child development centers and home settings charge. As a private contractor, it often is YOUR turn, your personal responsibility to claim the payment you agreed upon.

Reduce childcare costs by teaming up with another parent or two. You could take turns babysitting (outside your regular working hours, of course), or arrange for one parent to watch all the kids while the other(s) are at work. If everyone has the required clearances, it might pay additional dividends to look after a few other kids. This way, the sitter earns extra income without leaving their own child. For enough extra cash to send an older child to overnight summer camp, you could babysit seven other kids two days a week. Or babysit on only one Saturday night monthly and cover the entire cost of private violin lessons for one teen! Sound the trumpet, for financial victories have been claimed.

CHAPTER 6

Health Insurance and Medical Expenses

If you get hit with a huge medical expense, don't waste a moment mourning about it. Pick up the phone. Call the health care provider. Tell them you can pay a little bit and that you will make no worse than token payments for a few months. I know some divorcees who have had tens of thousands of dollars in hospital bills written off when they played the paupers in the manner I just described. The health care provider would rather take what they can get than go after you only to hit a stone wall with the extravagant costs that doctors and hospitals incur in a modern medical practice. Carefully check every medical bill to make sure it is always accurate. The sad fact is that doctors, dentists, and hospital record keepers make mistakes. Not usually intentionally, but they can and do make mistakes. Carefully check your bills every time. Medical services providers appreciate it when you catch and correct mistakes. At a family counseling session, we talked about the many mistakes clients had found in their bills.

I wish I could tell you there's an easy way to handle medical expenses as a single parent. I can't. But my advice is simple and straightforward. Get medical insurance for your kids, even if it means you can't afford it for yourself. Depending on your economic situation, your children may qualify for state programs. If you can't afford coverage for yourself, but you can afford it for your children, don't hesitate. Focus on their coverage. For yourself, visit free and reduced-cost health care facilities in your area. Some people are put off by this option, but remember, it is far better to be penniless and have health care for your kids than to be penniless and have none at all. Take care of your children first. Always remember, when you're a single parent, you are the glue that holds that family together. Be there for your kids, for your sake as well as theirs.

CHAPTER 7

Education and Extracurricular Activities

Another thing to consider is extracurricular activities. Public schools have music programs, clubs, AFT programs, a variety of sports, etc. available to their students. For students with interests that are not included in the school's selection, private and charter schools generally have a lower number of students and a tighter relationship between school administration and parents, which could give them more power when it comes to bringing in and funding an after-school activity. Homeschool students can take advantage of the extracurricular activities available for the entire city, not just the part of it specific to their own school. Additionally, homeschool students have more schedule freedom and more time to dedicate to training with a chosen private teacher in the areas of their interest. This type of investment is one of the advantages that could give homeschool students more opportunities for college admission in the difficult times of students competing for the same college seats. Smart budgeting for single parents involves finding a balance between expenses and money saved.

There are plenty of options available, including public schools, private schools, charter schools, home-based education, and online education. They all have their pros and cons, and different kinds of kids thrive in different settings. Private schools generally have more money to spend per student, a smaller student population, and could provide more challenging coursework. Charter schools are usually given some slack on their budget with the goal to give more freedom to the school's personnel. Think about what matters most to you. Homeschool and some online schools give schedule freedom and customization of courses while letting your child learn in a more comfortable, less stressful environment away from peer pressure. However, one advantage that public schools have over all other types of schools is the built-in social networks that automatically bring friendships and potential extracurricular activities.

CHAPTER 8

Building an Emergency Fund

Having an emergency fund can help prevent a financial disaster. But how do you plan on building this fund if you are a single parent struggling to ask for child support or to start a new career with no job experience? There are many things that you can do that will eliminate the need for this fund, such as searching for ways to get loans for bad credit, no credit check, and making money on the side. If you still decide to proceed with creating those funds, Sarah from California, and many other single parents took a simple step that involved paying themselves first. They took a percentage of their hard-earned paycheck and divided it into a separate account exclusively for this emergency fund. Then, Sarah made sure that she had set it to transfer money the day after payday. Before she could miss it, this money was diverted into her savings. Also, every time Sarah got a raise at work or invested in the stock market, she reassessed and increased the percentage of each paycheck that is saved.

Many financial experts recommend building an emergency fund as the very first step in developing a budget because it is your safety net against unexpected expenses and financial problems. Although most important, building an emergency fund is the easiest and hardest task you'll ever do. It's the easiest considering that you take a small amount of money from each paycheck and deposit it into a separate account. It's also the hardest considering it takes time and commitment to save that money without spending it. For example, Sarah from California mentions: "There are always unexpected expenses. My biggest advice to make a single mom budget work is to have an emergency fund." This fund should include 3-6 months' living expenses. So, if your living expenses are $2000/month, your emergency fund should total anywhere from $6000 - $12000. Otherwise, if you're a single parent with an income that fluctuates from month to month, like one who works in the gig economy, you should aim for 12 months' of living expenses rather than 3-6 months.

CHAPTER 9

Strategies for Debt Repayment

You are on your way. Follow this smart budgeting process, and be on your way to reducing every credit card, car loan, new water heater or that $2,000 loan from a friend. You're a Super Hero, and you will defeat debt. Keep your budget current, make the necessary changes, believe in yourself, keep your end goal top-of-mind. In just a short time, you will see those balances paid in full. Congratulations – you did it!

The strategies outlined here will provide incentive, excitement and a system to honestly assess debt, organize it into manageable chunks, and plan for the first installment. This debt reduction superhero will come to the rescue of your peace of mind and your pocketbook. While it's going to take time and effort, isn't your peace worth a few minutes each day?

Paying off debt can feel overwhelming if you don't have a plan in place. Debt is discouraging and severely hampers your ability to achieve financial freedom. Many single parents fall into the trap of debt. They may have turned to credit cards to make ends meet when money is tight, or they're on a restricted income due to a court-ordered child support or alimony payment. Regardless of the reasons, it's time to face the debt and put an end to it.

CHAPTER 10

Investing for the Future

He now earns a comfortable income and lives a frugal lifestyle, putting money into his 401K and some other investments. "My youngest sister turns 18 in another year - I'll be 50. If everything goes according to plan, I will retire at 56 and watch her while my parents are on a mission for our church. By the time they get home, my little sister will be 20 years old and the youngest three will all have college degrees (free because each of us also went to school on missions at the age of 19) and zero debt. I will have just paid off the mortgage on the home and will have the option to sell the home and downsize, using the proceeds to bump up the retirement funding. Then my siblings can use the previous property as a down payment if needed to get started on their own property."

Many single parents are not only focusing on short-term savings goals - like budgeting for the holidays or taking a trip with their kids - they also have an eye on the future and are focused on long-term financial goals too. Some of these longer-term goals include paying off debt, like a car loan or student loans, and saving for retirement too. Mark Foley is not only a single father, but one who is focused on long-term goals. He started saving for retirement right out of high school, he says. "I was a Boy Scout, and my mom taught my brothers and me the principles of compound interest using a $100 savings bond that we all each got when we were about three years old."

CHAPTER 11

Teaching Kids about Money

It's critical that your behavior supports your teaching about money. A kid who has no idea how to handle money is not going to grow into a financially savvy adult. Instead, a financially confused kid without a toolbox of money skills becomes a financially inept adult who can no longer fend for himself or others. As a good parent, you know you have to meet the needs of your children. While providing the latest hi-tech gadgets and made-to-the-nines designer jeans might meet the desires of your children, doing so without consideration of cost and the effects on your children's values and beliefs about money is not meeting anyone's needs. When we give our children things they don't understand, we build in them character traits that don't serve them well. That's because lowering expectations, which is the result of overindulging young people, denies them of the personal successes they need.

Once you start teaching your children about money, you have to be prepared to follow through in a consistent manner so they always know what you expect of them. As a single parent raising financially smart kids, you have a special role to fill: that of the primary money role model. Of course, kids will look at what you say and what you do. But they'll pay even more attention to the fact that you're in charge of money and that usually what you say goes. They'll listen - and learn - whether you're saying anything or not.

CHAPTER 12

Seeking Financial Assistance and Support

Speak with your child's other parent and lay down the fact that this is not about your relationship with your child together, this is about the life of your child. Make them understand that they are rearing an amazing little person and that by not contributing they are not doing their fair part in getting the resource he or she needs in order to grow up to be a well-adjusted, happy little human. You don't have to be confrontational or debate it – just present them with facts (your child's expenses and the fact that they're legally obligated to share them, often in much greater entirety in the short-term than in the long-term). If they don't abide at this point, seek legal support. Proficient legal professionals who specialize in family law will generally work with you to get your case sorted efficiently because they often will only make money when you do.

If you are not receiving child support that you are lawfully entitled to, put your pride or fears of confrontation aside to do what's right for your family. Don't allow your pride to hinder your financial ability to provide for your child. Your ability to provide for your children is the most important concern. If you are not receiving child support that your child's other parent is legally obligated to give, don't pawn to pride of wanting to do it alone. You can do it alone, and no one is questioning your abilities, but take help where help is willing to be given. In fact, fight to get what's rightfully yours when it comes to the well-being of your child.

CHAPTER 13

Balancing Work and Family Life

Another part of bringing balance is to make sure that everyone does get to have some time to themselves. Many single parents forget to take time for themselves and focus solely on the family. But if the primary parent is overworked and constantly run down, the family is going to see that and that's going to cause a ripple of negativity in the environment. It's okay to take a little time to yourself when the kids are in bed. If your budget allows, see if you can afford a baby-sitter for an hour a week. It's important to keep yourself in balance through all of this craziness. It's not always possible to keep things together, but with a little bit of effort and support (not to mention some creative fix-it tips to whip your house and vehicle into budget-friendly shape), things start to run a little more smoothly. Once you learn to find order, you start to see patterns to things and can better manage your time available. After all, the best time management skills are those that help keep your kids healthy and happy as well as successful in their lives.

These days, working single parents are very common. But just because it's an everyday occurrence doesn't mean it's easy. Many single parents are trying to work, manage the home and side jobs, and also raise children. Although it may seem like there's not a lot of time left over when all those other things are done, it's also a good idea to make an effort to spend quality time with your children. That little bit of extra one-on-one time can mean the world to them. One way to get things done is to involve them in it. When it's their turn to clean the house, make it a sort of contest to see who can sweep the floor the fastest or find all the dirty laundry. Then, once all the stuff is done, take the time to go play a game in the yard or watch a favorite show together. It may not be a lot, and you'll probably be super tired, but it's important to give them time and attention too.

CHAPTER 14

Self-Care and Stress Management

Work on your stress management every day. Show your children the importance of learning to manage stress by being a good role model for how to cope in a healthy way. Start by developing a list of things that calm you and help you vent. Explore what activities and thoughts calm you when you are stressed, such as prayer and meditation, listening to soft music at a low volume, preparing favorite meals or taking short leisurely walks. Simultaneously, input habits that help relieve stress in the house would be reflected on your children. Try making dinner time a relaxed affair instead of a struggle to keep food down. Eventually you'll notice that even though there are tough times, family members will seek that sequence of relief when stressed out. Children are naturally comforted by rituals, and when you set up a routine for indulging in activities that relieve stress every day, they internalize these activities to cope with personality issues, conflicts and existential stresses.

The stress level in single-parent households is potentially higher. There is a potential to feel emotionally stressed and overwhelmed by meeting family obligations as an earner and as a parent. Besides the sheer effort of meeting the demands of parenting solo, there may also be higher psychological and financial costs involved in maintaining connection and involvement with the non-resident partner and their extended families. That said, with good stress management, a single parent can make a secure, supportive unit where children can find a sense of emotional stability even in the absence of the other parent. There is considerable evidence to suggest that the availability of a single secure attachment relationship can mitigate the negative effects of stress.

CHAPTER 15

Building a Support
Network

Another chapter provides a list of sources for information and support on financial and legal matters such as estate planning and retirement savings, including the Employee Retirement Income Security Act (ERISA). Also discussed are Individual Development Accounts (IDAs) and Earned Income Tax Credit (EITC). The Internet is an outstanding resource for additional information not presented in the chapter, initially compiled in 2003, and the book provides current addresses and telephone numbers. Experts and parents discuss KeyBank's college savings account promoted on the EarnBenefits site and offer a cost comparison between the investment account H&R Block offers and Key Education Bank, promoted by the EarnBenefits site. Users find suggestions for creating and operationalizing online grocery shopping by reading of other parents' experiences in the "Spaghetti Lovers" (emphasis on balancing needs and entertainment) forum. By completing an assessment, in less than 15 minutes, one parent receives a list of health benefits to which he or she and the child are entitled. Besides the National

Resource Center for Working Families, three other members of the listed team provide support for single parents by giving suggestions for Loans and Grants and other assistance programs.

Single Parenthood Sourcebook, compiled by Cheryl Lee Price and others in 2003, provides single parents with a comprehensive overview of evidence-based resources specifically targeted to the needs of single-parent families. One chapter describes and evaluates empirical research studies designed to measure the impact of discipline techniques on children in single-parent families. Findings are presented which demonstrate that other people involved with the child, besides the single parent, appear to play a pivotal role in the child's ability to make the transition from a solitary to a two-parent family system. This chapter is comprised of lists of informational resources for the academic community and for additional books and periodicals.

CHAPTER 16

Planning for Retirement

The individual retirement account allows you to save a certain amount of money each year so it will generate interest on it, and unlike your 401k which is sponsored through work, you have a few different saving options. A traditional IRA is one that you must pay income tax in full on the money, and this is the money your investments multiply. A Roth IRA works the opposite way. You pay taxes on the money you put into it, but when it comes time to make a withdrawal (or draw), you don't need to pay a cent of tax on anything. Once again, you are going to want to save as much as you can, but don't feel bad if you have to start off small. If you max out your contribution early on in the year and you try to make an additional one, you run the risk of losing money on that extra money, so don't try to make all of your money back. Remember, every single dollar matters.

A 401k is a great retirement option to consider. While you may not think it is important to set money aside for this stage of your life now, you will certainly thank yourself later. The best aspect of a 401k is that money is directly withdrawn from your paycheck before you even get the chance to see it. Many large companies offer a Retirement Savings Plan, or RSP, where they will match a certain amount of the money you save for retirement. This is a great offering because it is essentially getting free money. You may not have thousands of dollars in it as many people do, but every single penny helps. It is also very risky to put all your savings in one place, especially in something that depends on the stock market. You never know how things will turn out, and retirement is a very important phase of your life where you should feel comfortable with the way things are going.

CHAPTER 17

Tax Planning for Single Parents

The Child Tax Credit is worth up to $2,000 per qualified child, age 16 or younger, for the income tax returns due July 15, 2020. The amount is per child and reduces the amount of tax owed. Additionally, for the income tax returns due July 15, 2020, you can claim a partial CTC of up to $500 per might-qualify-for-dependent if the Taxpayer Identification Number (TIN) you're using to claim them was issued by the due date of your return, as well. The credit begins to diminish for individuals with adjusted gross incomes of more than $200,000, or $400,000 or more for a married couple filing a joint return. Although the standard $2,000 per child is phased out in the three years following the year that a child turns 17, the phase out is still a difficult threshold. Therefore, single parents who are middle- and upper-income should neither rely on the Child Tax Credit as a source of emergency or retirement savings, nor rely on it to accommodate their needs in the same way they would their federal income tax withholding portion of their paychecks.

Whether you are a first-time filer, you have filed head of household before, or are experiencing a big life change, like a parental divorce, tax planning can make a significant difference in your refund. Single parents can claim the Head of Household status on their taxes. If they have minor kids, they may also be able to claim the Child Tax Credit, as well, meaning they can also endure a smaller tax burden. Working single parents—particularly those without the income from a former spouse—can use smart tax planning to lessen their tax burden and allot dollars they receive from their tax refunds in the wisest way.

CHAPTER 18

Estate Planning and Insurance

If you don't have a will, the court is going to appoint a guardian for your children regardless of whether you have a spouse or a partner or not. You want to make it very clear who you would like to be the guardian of your children. It also addresses choosing someone that you would like to be in charge of your children's inheritances. You can set that up in a trust. We're not getting into that much detail today, but it's really important for single parents to have a trust to manage on behalf of your children, which also outlines how those assets will be distributed to your kids after you're gone. Trusts are pretty flexible; they can be used during your lifetime as well. The final piece of doing that is once you set it all up, you'll want to talk to the people that you have appointed. If you have any minor children, you will need life insurance since they'll need to be provided for financially if you die. Having a guardian named in the will is important. It's not always legally binding, but it does give you a voice as to who you would like to have caring for your children if that's an important thing for you.

Dawn Doebler: It's not good for your family if you die without a will. You would be surprised how many single parents don't have a will that directs how their children should be cared for. That's the place I would always start. If you don't have one, please get a will, get it written. You can do it yourself online. You can start there, and then estate laws vary dramatically from state to state. So if you die, let's say, without a will, it's the state laws that determine pretty much everything. Whereas if you have a will, you can provide detailed instructions about how your estate should be handled, and that's your real voice talking from the grave.

Sheryl Nance-Nash: Let's go through these, starting with estate planning. Where do we start, why should we bother?

CHAPTER 19

Overcoming Financial Challenges

Many single parents become more thrifty than their married peers. They may cut expenses on various things but create huge debts if they don't face the root problem: inadequate income. That's why single parents can benefit from professional financial advice. Adults who have children, who don't have spouses, and who work have created special needs in crucial areas such as insurance, savings, and income enhancement. There are many programs and organizations that support single parents. Some offer college scholarships, some provide daycare services for very moderate fees, some help with housing, job search, or legal issues. Hop onto the Internet and check the services that are available in your area. There may be a federal program or a city institution that can strengthen your safety net. One last idea: knowledge, they say, is power. It's well-documented that poverty among single parents in America is defined and self-perpetuating. Don't let it happen to you. Control rationally your spending and plan financially, that's for sure, but manage your budget to improve free time, which you should devote to learning and career building. Work out a plan that not only makes you more money today but also should, over the years, climb you up the income scale, which will then improve your living standard and ease the strain that currently may hurt you, your kids, their education, and their future.

You're a single parent and you can't do anything right. Your two-year-old is screaming and your kindergartener has hijacked a grocery cart and is on his way to the candy aisle. You're dead on your feet after a 10-hour day and to top it off, you have this never-ending feeling that you're not doing enough to give your kids what they deserve. Does it sound familiar? You bet it does. Some 48 million women in America raised at least one child under 18 years of age last year. Each of these women can relate to the miseries I've sketched or worse. Single parents know very well how difficult it is to maintain a family when they're facing chronic shortages in time, money, and support. Add to that the death of a partner, divorce, and the resulting stress and loneliness, and you have an extraordinary achievement at hand every time you feed, clean, dress, get on a school bus, or soothe to sleep one of your kids. The silver lining is that parents often show young people a healthy way to live with difficulties.

CHAPTER 20

Celebrating Financial Successes

Make sure that as your children get older and have increasingly more complex money questions, you tell them about your money thought processes when they're ready. Show them how you build your budget, what your financial goals are, how you track them, and what actions you took to correct things when you started to go off plan. Sit down and thoroughly explain these things when they ask. These lessons are vital as they grow and begin making their own money choices. Long before they've crossed the threshold into their adult lives, your children will have learned the lessons of responsibly budgeting from your guidance and example.

Creating a culture of celebrating financial wins with your children is a wonderful way to reinforce healthy money habits. If you've hit the savings goal you've been working toward, reach out to your child's other parent to come over and celebrate with the whole family. In planning and being frugal, don't forget to talk about what's happening so that your children understand and buy into the idea of choosing to live this way. For a child that has never lived with their other parent, the financial constraints should be shared in an age-appropriate, neutral way that makes clear that neither you nor they are to "blame"; it's an outcome of decisions and events that were not under either of your control.

CHAPTER 21

Conclusion

In summary, single parents can weather the financial storm and build a happy and healthy family by sticking strictly to the budget, understanding essential family needs, eliminating debts, and carefully organizing the finance. All those things may be achieved through structured mental processes and an action plan specifically prepared for single parents. It begins and ends with setting clear goals, closely monitoring the progress, making necessary adjustments, and cutting unnecessary expenses or affording bills. During these tough economic times, learning to adjust with the changing environment is a crucial element to maintain the family's financial stability in the world dynamic markets or any financial market.

The role of a single parent is not easy, especially when shouldering the responsibilities of providing a well-rounded childhood for their child. A single parent often faces several obstacles and challenges as the only source of financial support for their child. As such, a smart budget should be within the sights of every single parent. A smart budget is a spending plan that ensures everything needed by the family is taken care of and any unplanned or unexpected setbacks do not have a serious detrimental effect on the family's financial stability. The money made by single parents will go further with a smart budget. This will result in stress reduction, increased savings, and improved control over finance.

www.ingramcontent.com/pod-product-compliance
Ingram Content Group UK Ltd.
Pitfield, Milton Keynes, MK11 3LW, UK
UKHW042029171224
452550UK00010B/174